CAT FACTS

Tabitha Jones

Gramercy Books
New York

This 2001 edition is published by Gramercy Books™, an imprint of Random House Value Publishing, Inc. 280 Park Avenue, New York, N.Y. 10017.

Gramercy Books™ and design are trademarks of Random House Value Publishing, Inc.

Random House
New York • Toronto • London • Sydney • Auckland
http://www.randomhouse.com/

Design by Robert Yaffe

Printed and bound in China

Library of Congress Cataloging-in-Publication Data

Jones, Tabitha, 1972-
    Cat facts / Tabitha Jones.
        p. cm.
    ISBN 0-517-20807-5
        1. Cats—Miscellanea. I. Title.

SF445.5 J66 2001
636.8—dc21

                                    00-057837

9 8 7 6 5 4 3 2 1

Contents

CAT FACTS

**Books of similar interest from
Random House Value Publishing**

The Big Book of Cats

Cat Tales

How to Live with a Neurotic Cat

How to Talk to Your Cat

Instant Guide to Cats

The Mysterious, Magical Cat

No Naughty Cats

365 Ways to Love Your Cat

Facts, Quirky and Otherwise

More than 35,000 kittens are born
in the United States each year.

There are an estimated 65-70 million cats
in the United States in about
32 million households.

According to the year 2000 estimates, 25% of all
United States households have at least one cat. The
number is expected to grow another 5% between
2000 and 2010. Cats have surpassed dogs as the
most popular domestic pet.

According to a Gallup poll, most American
pet owners obtain their cats by adopting strays.

The most popular breed in the U.S. is
the Persian, a long-haired cat. The most
popular short-haired cat is the Siamese.

It is estimated that 25% of all cat
owners in the U.S. blow dry their cat's hair
after a bath.

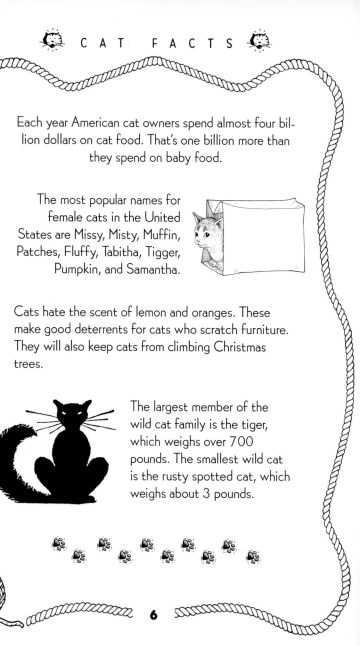

Each year American cat owners spend almost four billion dollars on cat food. That's one billion more than they spend on baby food.

The most popular names for female cats in the United States are Missy, Misty, Muffin, Patches, Fluffy, Tabitha, Tigger, Pumpkin, and Samantha.

Cats hate the scent of lemon and oranges. These make good deterrents for cats who scratch furniture. They will also keep cats from climbing Christmas trees.

The largest member of the wild cat family is the tiger, which weighs over 700 pounds. The smallest wild cat is the rusty spotted cat, which weighs about 3 pounds.

The fastest land animal is a wild cat, the cheetah, clocked at over 60 mph. The cheetah does not have retractable claws, as do most other cats.

The Cat Fanciers' Association International Cat Show, held annually the weekend before Thanksgiving at various U.S. locations, is the largest international pedigreed cat show in the Western Hemisphere. The three-day event showcases nearly 1,300 pedigreed cats from all over the world.

The "catgut" that was used for strings in tennis rackets and musical instruments does not come from cats. It actually comes from sheep, hogs, and horses. The only time actually cat gut was used was by Japanese geishas, who used catgut for the strings of their samisen.

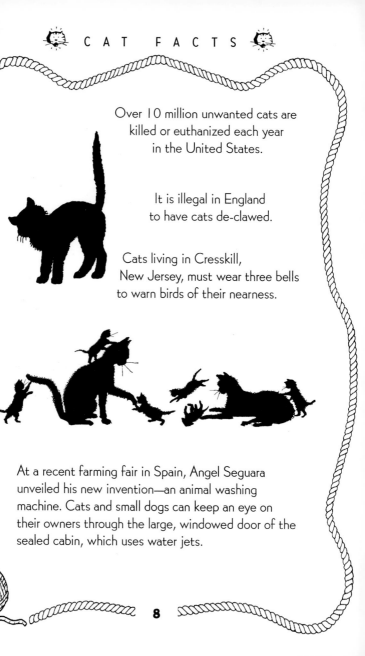

Over 10 million unwanted cats are
killed or euthanized each year
in the United States.

It is illegal in England
to have cats de-clawed.

Cats living in Cresskill,
New Jersey, must wear three bells
to warn birds of their nearness.

At a recent farming fair in Spain, Angel Seguara
unveiled his new invention—an animal washing
machine. Cats and small dogs can keep an eye on
their owners through the large, windowed door of the
sealed cabin, which uses water jets.

Forty percent of cat owners carry pictures of their pets in their wallets.

The average cat food meal is the equivalent to about five mice.

In 1978, a British cat had the longest tail on record, measuring in at a whopping fourteen inches.

From Teeth to Tail

A domestic cat's skeleton has at least 230 bones.
Humans have 206 bones. This is why cats are
extremely flexible.

The average cat
weighs 12 pounds.
If you cannot feel a cat's ribs,
it is too heavy.

According to the *Guinness Book of World Records*,
the heaviest cat, an Australian cat named Himmy,
weighed 46 pounds 15.25 ounces when recorded in
1986. The previous record-holder had been Spice, a
ginger and white American
tomcat who was weighed in
at 43 pounds in 1977.

The tiniest cat on record
was a male Himalayan-
Persian named Tinker Toy from Illinois. He weighed
1 pound 8 ounces, was 7-1/4" long and 2-3/4 " tall.

A cat can jump five times as high as it is tall.

Cats, along with giraffe and camels, are the only animals that walk by moving both their left feet and then both their right feet. This helps with their speed and agility. A domestic cat can sprint at about 31 miles per hour.

A cat's tongue is covered with filiform, an abrasive surface. It is an excellent tool for scraping fat and meat off prey, and also acts as a sponge for absorbing liquids. It also makes a good grooming brush.

Normal body temperature for a cat is 101.5 to 102°F, slightly warmer than humans.

Cats take between 20-40 breaths a minute.

The only one who can safely pick up a kitten by the scruff of its neck is its own mother.

A kitten does not begin to develop eyesight until it is
about two weeks old. It begins to
walk at about 20 days.

Cats hearts beat almost twice as fast a
human hearts, about 110 to 140
beats per minute. An excited cat's
heart rate can climb to 240
beats per minute.

Cats can see up to 120 feet away with peripheral
vision of about 285 degrees. Cats can see color, but
they are believed to have some of the characteristics
of color blindness. Cats do not see detail very well.

Cats can see in the dark about six times better than
humans. They have an extra layer of reflecting cells,
called a *tapetum lucidum*. These cells also give cats'
eyes a strange glow when light hits them.

A cat has approximately 60 to 80
olfactory cells, which explains their
sensitive sense of smell. Humans
have between 6 and 20 million
olfactory cells.

Most cats have four toes on their hind feet and five on the front. But some cats have extra toes—as many as seven or eight on one foot. These cats are called *poly-dactyl.*

Most white cats with two blue eyes are deaf.

Cats need five times more protein in their diets than do dogs.

Almost 10% of a cat's bones are in its tail, which is used to maintain balance.

Cats eyes come in three shapes: round, slanted, and almond. Most cats do not have eyelashes.

C A T   F A C T S

Cats have a third eyelid called
a "haw" that covers their eyes from injury.

A cat's ear has 30 muscles, many of which
control movement. A cat's ear can pivot
180° and can turn in the direction of
sound faster than a good watchdog.

An adult cat has 32 teeth, the fewest teeth of all car-
nivores. It has no grinding teeth so it must tear its
food. Cats have no wisdom teeth.

A cat bite is more likely to become infected than a
dog bite, but neither is as dangerous as a human bite
because humans have far more bacteria
in their mouths.

Whiskers are used as sensory
devices, detecting air currents,
animal movement, and judging
space. Cats have 24 movable
whiskers, 12 on each side.

Male cats usually mark 10 times
more territory than females.

A cat's nose pad is ridged in a unique pattern,
just like human fingerprints.

Only 40% of cats are
ambidextrous. Most
cats are either "righty"
or "lefty."

A female cat is able to have more than 100 kittens
during the length of her productive life. An average
cat has 1 to 8 kittens per litter and has two to
three litters a year.

The gestation
period for a cat is
about 65 days.

Neutering a cat can
extend its life span by two
or three years.

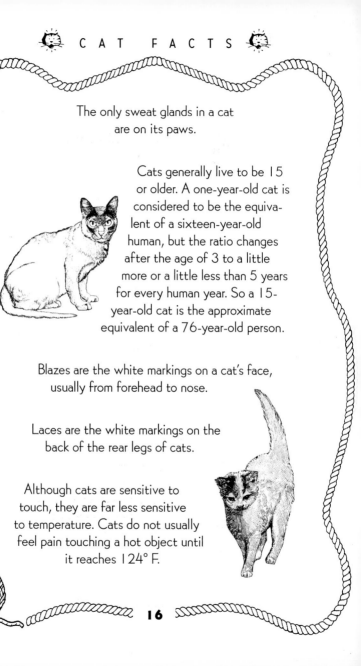

The only sweat glands in a cat
are on its paws.

Cats generally live to be 15
or older. A one-year-old cat is
considered to be the equivalent of a sixteen-year-old
human, but the ratio changes
after the age of 3 to a little
more or a little less than 5 years
for every human year. So a 15-
year-old cat is the approximate
equivalent of a 76-year-old person.

Blazes are the white markings on a cat's face,
usually from forehead to nose.

Laces are the white markings on the
back of the rear legs of cats.

Although cats are sensitive to
touch, they are far less sensitive
to temperature. Cats do not usually
feel pain touching a hot object until
it reaches 124° F.

A cat can have as many as 200 hairs per square millimeter of skin.

Cats have inner ear canals that help them land on their feet.

The domestic cat is the only cat species able to hold its tail vertically while walking. All wild cats hold their tails horizontally or tucked between their legs while walking.

Cats have 290 bones in their bodies and 517 muscles.

There are three body types for a cat. *Cobby* type is a compact body, deep chest, short legs, and broad head. The eyes are large and round. *Muscular* type is a sturdy body and round, full-cheeked head. *Foreign* type is a slender body, with long legs and a long tail. The head is wedge-shaped, with tall ears and slanting eyes.

The Cat's Meow or Cat Purrsonalities

Most cats love high places—especially leopards and jaguars who sleep in trees.

Domestic cats are loners, but when placed in a group they can learn to share space, especially if there is plenty of food for all.

Cats spend 16 hours of each day sleeping. They are more active during the evening.

Cats knead with their paws when they're happy.

Cats love to chew on grass, catnip, parsley and sage. But beware that many other plants are toxic to cats.

A cat will almost never "meow" at another cat. This is reserved for humans.

A cat that snores or rolls over on his back to expose his belly trusts its environment.

Gentle head butts into arms or legs are a cat's sign of affection.

Cats use their tails as communicators. When greeting a person or another animal it likes, the cat will raise its tail straight up. It may quiver with delight and then wrap itself around the person. If a cat faces possible conflict, the tail will be vertical and slightly bushed out. If the tension increases, the tail will whip from side to side. If it is fearful, the tail is lowered and fuzzed. Real anger is expressed by a tail swishing violently from side to side. A tail flick is the same as thumbing one's nose, an insulting gesture.

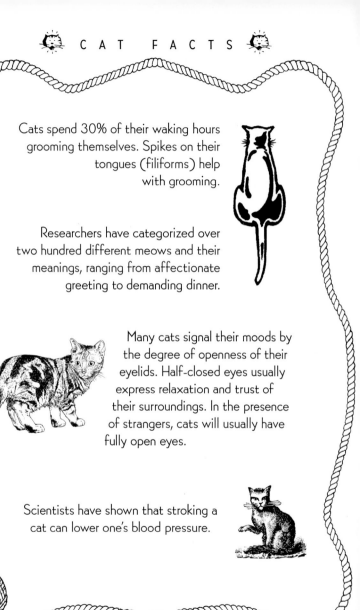

Cats spend 30% of their waking hours grooming themselves. Spikes on their tongues (filiforms) help with grooming.

Researchers have categorized over two hundred different meows and their meanings, ranging from affectionate greeting to demanding dinner.

Many cats signal their moods by the degree of openness of their eyelids. Half-closed eyes usually express relaxation and trust of their surroundings. In the presence of strangers, cats will usually have fully open eyes.

Scientists have shown that stroking a cat can lower one's blood pressure.

Cats have been known to react to stress experienced by their owners by excessive licking and fur pulling.

It is believed that nervous adult cats were not handled enough in their first eight weeks of life.

Many cats will try to get a person's attention when they are talking on the telephone because they do not see anyone else in the room and think you are talking to them.

Cats seem to have perfect pitch and will often leave the room if a singer or musician is performing off-key.

Siamese (and part Siamese) cats are usually more outgoing and active than Persian, who are more sedate. They also love climbing.

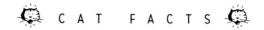

It is natural for cats to eat grass. They do this not only to facilitate throwing up fur balls and other ingested but indigestible items, but also because they occasionally enjoy a "salad."

If your cat is near you, and her tail is quivering, this is an expression of affection. If her tail starts thrashing, run for cover.

Cats prefer their food at room temperature, and will absolutely REFUSE to eat any food that is too hot or too cold.

22

Cat Hisstory

The cat goddess Bastet—whose name was also spelled Bast, Pasht, and many other ways—became one of the most sacred of all figures worshipped by the Egyptians. She was represented with the head of a cat. Soon all cats became sacred to the Egyptians, and all were well cared for.

Cats were first tamed for use as rodent and pest control in Egypt around 3000 BC. They soon became household pets that were given great status.

The Ancient Egyptian god Ra, the god of light, was often referred to as the Great Cat.

Cats born in May were usually drowned, since they were thought to be poor mousers, hunting only glowworms and snakes.

Cats were tortured and sometimes burned alive during the Spanish Inquisition when they were considered representatives of the devil.

The Mau is named for its Egyptian ancestry's word for cat. The Mau is the only natural domestic spotted breed and is believed to be a subspecies of the

African wild cat. Tomb hieroglyphics found on the walls of the pyramids depict this spotted cat as domesticated more than 4,000 years ago. The Mau first arrived in the United States in 1956.

In Ancient Egypt, family members shaved their eyebrows in mourning when the family cat died.

In ancient Egypt, killing a cat was a crime punishable by death.

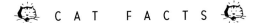

In one ancient city in Egypt, more than 300,000 cat mummies were found. Embalmed mice were usually placed with them in their tombs.

In Europe, cats were buried under fruit trees to increase the growth of the fruit.

In the Middle Ages, cats in Europe were persecuted because they were thought to possess demonic power. Some historians believe that the absence of cats in Europe contributed to the outbreak of the Great Plague.

In France in the Middle Ages, ceramic cats were put on rooftops to ward off evil. Although today people don't believe this any more, many homes in France still have ceramic cats on their roofs.

The Pilgrims were the first to introduce cats to North America.

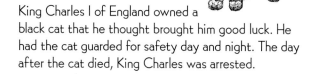

In the sixteenth century, a visitor to an English home would always kiss the family cat to bring good luck.

King Charles I of England owned a black cat that he thought brought him good luck. He had the cat guarded for safety day and night. The day after the cat died, King Charles was arrested.

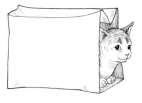

The Kit-Cat Club, formed in London in the eighteenth century, was a gathering of literary figures, wealthy aristocrats, politicians, and even royalty. Goings-on at the Club were a bit mysterious, but it was said that many political, financial, and literary deals were forged there. Portraits of its members hang in the National Portrait Gallery in London.

The first formal cat show was held in England in 1871 at the Crystal Palace in London. The first formal cat show in America was held at Madison Square Garden in New York City in 1895.

Charles Bullard was the first American photographer of cats. He began his work in about 1887.

Latham Foundation for the Humane Education, founded by the Latham family of philanthropists in 1918, was the first to honor distinguished cats in the 1920s.

PATSY awards, Picture Animal Top Star Awards, were first presented at the American Humane Society of Los Angeles in 1951. Winners have included Pyewacket in *Bell, Book and Candle,*

CAT FACTS

Rhubarb in *Breakfast at Tiffany's*, and Tonto in *Harry and Tonto*. Morris also won a PATSY award for his cat food commercials.

Kitty litter was invented in 1947 when a neighbor complained to Edward Lowe about using ashes as filler in her cat's box, and what a mess it made. Lowe worked for his father's company in Michigan, which sold industrial absorbents including an absorbent clay called Fuller's Earth. Lowe suggested using the clay to his neighbor. The neighbor loved it. Lowe decided to package this new cat box filler, called it Kitty Litter, and brought it to a local store. In spite of the store's reluctance to carry it, Kitty Litter was a big success. Lowe started promoting his litter at cat shows and pet shops around the country. The rest is history. By 1990, Edward Lowe Industries, Inc. was the nation's largest producer of cat box filler, with retail sales of more than $210 million dollars annually. The Edward Lowe Foundation, founded by Lowe and now administered by his wife, advises and nurtures American entrepreneurs.

The oldest cat on record was Puss, in England, who died in 1939 just after her 36th birthday.

Sir Isaac Newton, who discovered the principles of gravity, also invented the cat door.

The record number for "mouse kills" is held by a tortoise-shell cat who worked on rodent control in Scotland. Towser killed about 28, 899 mice in her 21-year lifetime, which ended in 1987. This is about 4 mice a day.

According to the *Guinness Book of World Records*, the largest inheritance left to a cat was $415,000 to two cats in the 1960s. The richest inheritance by a single cat was $250,000.

The first Siamese cat brought to the
United States was a gift to President
Rutherford B. Hayes.

In 1972, the city of La Paz,
Bolivia, put 2000 "soldier cats"
into action to combat
a contagious fever carried by
rodents in the jungle.

In 1936, a 220-yard circuit was used as a cat-
racing track, and over 50 felines would chase
after an electric mouse.

Myths and Legends

 Ancient Celts believed that cats' tails had a mystical power. In fact, they believed that if you stepped on a cat's tail you would be bitten by a snake.

Many believe that seeing a cat sleeping with all four paws tucked under means that cold weather is coming.

When a cat's whiskers droop, rain is on its way.

If it rains on a Wednesday, it's because you forgot to feed the cat.

Calling a cat a "familiar" came from the medieval superstition that Satan's favorite form was a black cat. Witches were said, therefore, to have a cat as their "familiar."

The Birman, considered one of the most beautiful cat breeds, is also know as the "Sacred Cat of Burma," and has several legends about its origins. One is that

raiders killed a much-loved Khmer priest in Asia while he was in worship. His beautiful white temple cat, named Sinh, placed his paws on his master and faced the golden, goddess with sapphire blue eyes to which its master had been praying. The cat's white hair turned golden, his yellow eyes to sapphire, his legs earth brown, but his paws, which rested on his master stayed pure white. Birmans today look exactly the same.

In Japan, many believe that cats can cure melancholia and epilepsy.

Tuberculosis can be cured by wearing
the skin of a cat across the chest.

It's good luck if a stray cat
follows you.

It's bad luck to step on a cat.

If a cat sneezes near a bride on her wedding day,
she will have a happy marriage.

If a dark colored cat crosses your path,
it will bring you gold.

If a light colored cat crosses your path,
it will bring you silver.

Common cures for ridding
oneself of bad luck caused
by a cat crossing your path
include walking back thirteen
steps, turning around clockwise
three times, and throwing salt
over your left shoulder.

Stepping over a cat
brings bad luck.

If a cat passes over a dead
body in the house, the corpse
will become a vampire and
haunt you.

Some Japanese used to believe that a black patch on
a cat's back was a sacred mark, indicating the presence of an ancestor's soul.

Dreaming about a ginger cat brings luck
in money and business.

Dreaming about a tabby brings good luck
to your home.

Dreaming of a
tortoise shell cat
brings good luck in
love.

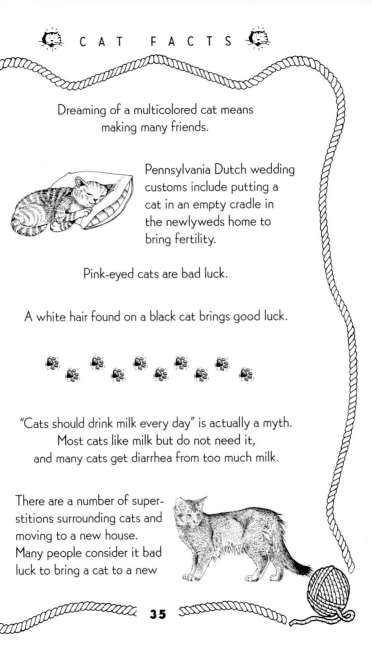

Dreaming of a multicolored cat means
making many friends.

Pennsylvania Dutch wedding
customs include putting a
cat in an empty cradle in
the newlyweds home to
bring fertility.

Pink-eyed cats are bad luck.

A white hair found on a black cat brings good luck.

"Cats should drink milk every day" is actually a myth.
Most cats like milk but do not need it,
and many cats get diarrhea from too much milk.

There are a number of super-
stitions surrounding cats and
moving to a new house.
Many people consider it bad
luck to bring a cat to a new

home. Others think that you can avoid the bad luck by putting the cat through the window rather than the door. For others, it is enough to let the cat into the house before you enter to avoid bad luck.

There is a legend that the only animal not invited to Buddha's funeral was the cat. This is because the mouse (or rat) that was sent to get medicine to save Buddha's life was killed by a cat on the way.

Many sailors believe that a cat on board ship means a lucky trip.

Some believe that it's bad luck if your cat has an uneven number of kittens.

When Indonesians want it to rain, they pour a little water over a cat's back.

Buttering a cat's feet will keep it from straying.

Cats do not have nine lives. It only seems that way because they have the ability to survive unhurt from falls, even falls of more than 40 feet.

In Great Britain, black cats are thought to bring good luck, not bad luck.

Some tribes in Africa's Ghana believe that a person passes into a cat's body at the moment of death.

The Kilkenny Cats are legendary Irish cats. It is believed that they fought until only their tails remained.

Kicking a cat causes rheumatism to develop in that leg.

If a farmer kills a cat, his cattle will die mysteriously.

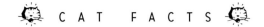

Breeds

There are more than 500 million domestic cats in the world, with almost 100 different breeds.

The ancestor of all domestic cats is the African Wild Cat, which still exists today.

Calico cats are almost always female.

The most popular breed of cat in the United States is the Persian, with over 45,000 registered in the country.

The Russian Blue is a natural breed, thought to have come from Russia. It is believed that they actually originated in Scandinavia. The breed has gone through various names such as Archangel, Maltese, Foreign Blue and Russian Blue. Fur trading and shipping may have had some bearing on their ability to be located in all these countries. The name has always been Russian Blue in North America.

The largest domestic cat breed is the Ragdoll. They are slow-maturing and are not full size until three years old, but males weigh 12 to 20 pounds, and females weigh 10 to 15 pounds. Ragdolls have large, oval, blue eyes, and are named for the way then tend to go limp when held, appearing quite laid back and placid. The breed was developed in the 1960s in California by breeding Persian, Birman, and Burmese.

Scottish Fold Cats are so named as they have both ears "folded" forward. They are similar in shape to British Shorthairs, and come in many colors. Scottish Folds have many unusual habits, such as sleeping on their backs or sitting up on their haunches like dogs.

The Japanese Bobtail has existed in Japan for at least 1000 years. Its most distinguishing characteristic is its naturally short tail, which looks like a bunny tail.

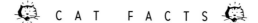

The Maine Coon cat is America's only natural breed of domestic cat. There are some myths that say that it originated by interbreeding the American bobcat with other Eastern seaboard cats, and others that claim its ancestors came from Norwegian cats brought over by the Vikings. One myth attributes its appearance in America to Captain Samuel Clough who had planned to smuggle Queen Marie Antoinette out of France to Maine, and when the plot failed and he had to sail without her, six of her favorite cats were already on board and made their way to America. Probably the Main Coon was brought to America by settlers.

The Singapura is the smallest breed of cat. It was brought to the United States by Americans who had been living in Singapore in the 1970 and brought three stray cats they had adopted there.

The domestic Bengal cat has a wild looking conformation and spotted and marble markings related to its distant Asian leopard cat ancestors. Bengals are considered real "people" cats, able to walk on a leash, fetch toys, and even talk. They are very popular and are also used for visiting hospices and nursing homes.

The Manx Cat is believed to have originated on the Isle of Man in England. There is much folklore about why the Manx is tailless, ranging from Noah shutting the cat's tail in the door of the Ark, or that tailless cats were brought from Japan to the Isle of Man by Phoenicians traders.

The Sphynx appears hairless, but it is covered with an extrememly fine down that feels like suede. This makes the Sphynx vulnerable to cold weather and sunburn, and it is considered strictly an indoor cat.

The head of a Sphynx is small with large triangular ears rounded at the tips, and its personality is very affectionate. The Sphynx is extremely rare, which makes them an expensive breed.

The Abyssinian, one of the most popular short hair breeds, is also one of the oldest known breeds. It is thought that the Abyssinian was present in Ancient Egypt, and many  paintings and sculptures resemble the Abyssinian. Another places its origins in Ethiopia, formerly Abyssinia. There is also a history that relates the origin of the breed to the Indian Ocean and parts of Southeast Asia. The first Abyssinian imported to North America from England arrived in the early 1900s.

One of the earliest known breeds in the world, and probably the purest, is the Korat. This cat with silver-blue short

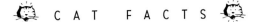
hair and luminous green eyes is thought to have origi-
nated in the jungles of the Malay Peninsula. The name
originated when King
Rama V of Siam was pre-
sented with the cat and
asked its origin. When he
was told that it came
from Korat, a high
plateau in north-
east Thailand, the

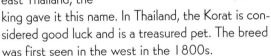

king gave it this name. In Thailand, the Korat is considered good luck and is a treasured pet. The breed
was first seen in the west in the 1800s.

Although not an accepted breed,
the California Spangled Cat, which
was bred to resemble a spotted
wild cat is a designer cat, featured
in the Neiman Marcus catalogue in
the early 1990s.

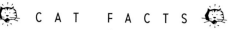

The Havana Brown cat is not of Cuban origin. It is a recently developed breed that originated in Great Britain. It is a distinctive type of oriental short hair with a chocolate coat. Some say it was named after a rabbit of the same color and others believe it got its breed name because it was the color of a fine Havana cigar. Brown cats have been known for centuries and their origins can probably be traced to Southeast Asia as a branch of the Royal Cats of Siam.

The Lake Van cat is an ancient breed that originated in central and southwest Asia, and took its name from a lake in Turkey. They are white, semi-longhaired cats with distinctive markings on their head, ears, and bushy tail. Unlike other domestic breeds, Vans love to swim.

In 1981, the American Curl made its first appearance by natural genetic alteration when a kitten in California was born with curled ears. They were first accepted as a breed several years later after breeders found that they were very hardy cats with no genetic abnormalities. A Curl is born with large, straight ears, which begin to curl back during the first week. The next few weeks the ears are tightly curled until about four months when they are set permanently. The degree of curl is now a breed show standard.

Famous Cats

The famous finicky Morris the Cat has actually been three different cats. The first Morris was originally named "Lucky" when he was adopted from a shelter in 1968 to be used in food commercials. The two cats used after his death in 1978 were also taken from shelters.

Puss 'n' Boots is a literary cat that wears boots, is very clever, and tricks people. He has appeared in fairy tales, stories, and animation.

Garfield, Jim Davis' famous creation, is big business, with his own website, television show, and plans for a theme park, Garfield's Adventure America.

Felix the Cat is one of cartoon's
most famous cats. He was created
by Otto Messmer in 1919.
Felix was the first cat to star
in a "talkie" cartoon.

Catbert is the name of comic-star Dilbert's
evil Human Resources Director.

The name of the
gray housecat in the
movie *Babe* was
Dutchess.

Lewis Carroll's Cheshire
Cat can disappear, leaving
only its grin showing.

Edgar Allan Poe, author of the
horror story, "The Black Cat"
was known to take his cat,
Catarina, everywhere
he went. The name
of the cat in the
story was Pluto.

Mohammed loved his cat Muessa so much, that it is said that he cut off his robe rather than disturb her when she was sleeping on it.

One of Barbie's kittens was named Fluff. Another one was named Honey.

Jones, the orange cat in *Alien*, was the only survivor besides Sigorney Weaver.

Dennis the Menace, created by Hank Ketcham, had a cat named Hot Dog.

The cartoon character Heathcliff, orange with black stripes, was named for the character in *Wuthering Heights*. His girlfriend's name is Sonia.

"Andy's Gang" was a popular television show in the 1950s and one of the most beloved characters was Midnight the Cat who told stories and introduced segments of the show.

Cat Ballou, the movie starring Jane Fonda as Cat Ballou and Lee Marvin, was awarded several Oscar nominations in 1965.

Baseball Hall of Famer Jim "Catfish" Hunter, pitched for the Kansas City Athletics and the Yankees. It was manager Charles O. Finley who gave him this nickname, making up a story about Hunter running away from home to go fishing and landing a catfish.

Stephen King's novel *Pet Sematary* begins with the death and burial of a cat named Church.

Elvis Presley was once known as "The Hillbilly Cat."

John Lennon's cat was named Elvis.

Sylvester, the black-and-white cartoon cat, was repeatedly tricked by Tweety Pie the canary. No matter how he tried, he always ended up crying "sufferin' succotash!" at the moment of defeat. His first appearance was in 1945.

Socks, the First Cat of the Clinton White House, had his own fan club, including a newsletter, covering the White House news from a cat's eye view, website, toys, gifts, his own ZIP code, and several published books including *Dear Socks, Dear Buddy, Children's Letters to Socks: Kids Write to America's 'First Cat'*, *Socks the Cat who Moved to Washington*, and *First Cat, Second Term: Socks Pussyfoots His Way Back into the White House.*

Cats, Andrew Lloyd Weber's musical based on T. S. Eliot's poems in *Old Possum's Book of Practical Cats*, holds the record as Broadway's longest-running musical.

Elizabeth Taylor had a cat named Jeepers Creepers.

Cleopatra had a cat named Charmian.

Slippers, Theodore Roosevelt's cat, had six toes on each foot.
His other cat, Tom Quartz, was named after the cat in Mark Twain's *Roughing It*.
It is said that Slippers attended many White House state dinners.

Tabby, the cat that belonged to Abraham Lincoln's son, Tad, lived in the White House.

Puff is the name of the cat in the reader *Fun with Dick and Jane*.

In *That Darn Cat*, a Walt Disney film in 1965, the lead character was played by a Siamese named Syn Cat. In the 1997 remake of the movie, it was played by a gray and white tabby named Elvis.

The Incredible Journey, a very popular movie made in 1963, told the story of a Siamese cat who joins up with a Labrador retriever and a bull terrier on a 250-mile trek across Canada, and the entire movie is from the animals' points of view.

The Adventures of Milo & Otis was a delightful movie about a trouble-prone kitten named Milo and Otis the pug who joins her on many adventures.

The Springfield Cat burglar from *The Simpsons* is named Malloy.

On the original *Batman* television series, the villain Catwoman was played by Lee Merriwether. Both Julie Newmar and Eartha Kitt also played the role. In the movie, the role was played by Michelle Pfeiffer.

An old English story, *Dick Whittington's Cat*, was about a poor orphan boy's companion and friend. After many mishaps and adventures, Dick became the Lord Mayor of London.

The comic strip character *Krazy Kat*, drawn by George Herriman, was first syndicated in 1911. Krazy Kat's sidekick was Ignatz the mouse.

Peter Sellers starred as Inspector Clouseau in *The Pink Panther* films, featuring a totally cool animated cat named The Pink Panther.

Ernest Hemingway owned 30 cats. The names of some of his cats were Ecstasy, Dillinger, Crazy Christian, Fats, Friendless Brother, Thruster, Willy, Whitehead, and Skunk.

Albert Schweitzer was left-handed but often used his right hand to write rather than disturb his cat Sizi who slept in the crook of his left arm.

The Cat in the Hat is one of Dr. Seuss's best known characters.

Don Marquis's *Archie and Mehitabel*, published during the 1930s, is based on correspondence between two friends, Archie, the alley cat, and Mehitabel, the cockroach.

Cardinal Richelieu, the most powerful person in France during the reign of Louis XIII, owned a black angora cat named Lucifer.

The 17th century writer Dr. Samuel Johnson, supposedly fed his favorite cat, Hodge, fresh oysters.

Tom and Jerry are among the most enduring characters of cartoons. The duo began in 1940 and are still going strong, the cat Tom and Jerry the mouse beloved by young and old alike.

Curiosity Killed the Cat, and Other Expressions

Ailurophilia is the "love of cats."

Ailurophobia is the fear of cats.

"The cat's meow" is a twentieth century expression for something very new—and popular.

In the eighteenth century, when piglets were sold in the market in small tied bags, sellers of piglets often would substitute a cat and pretend it was a pig. If the cat managed to escape, then the scam was revealed, giving rise to the expression, "Let the cat out of the bag." This market trick then became the source of another expression: "Don't buy a pig in a poke (bag)."

The "Cat's Pajamas," the term for remarkable or perfect, was first used in 1902 soon after the invention of pajamas, which were considered an incredible "invention."

A group of kittens is called a kindle.

A group of cats is called a clowder,
probably a variation of "clutter."

A gaycat is the nickname for a safecracker.

A cat caper is slang for a
despicable crime.

A cat burglar describes
a thief who is light on his feet, has great agility,
can climb easily, and has other
cat-like qualities.

"Give the cat another goldfish" is
a phrase originating in the 1940s
which means, "Let's splurge."

"Curiosity killed the cat" is a modern version of a sixteenth century proverb "care kills a cat," which was used to say that "care" or "worry" is bad for your health.

"Don't wake a sleeping cat" is the Italian version of "Let sleeping dogs lie."

A hep cat is someone who keeps up with the latest trends.

"It's raining cats and dogs." This term supposedly originated in ancient times when draining systems were poor and stray animals drowned in heavy storms. It may also have derived from the Greek word catadupa, which means waterfall.

The phrase "cat on a hot tin roof" originated from the British phrase, "like a cat on hot bricks. The name applies to someone who is nervous and jumpy, behaving as a cat would on a very hot roof. Its use in the play of the same name written by Tennessee Williams made it a famous expression.

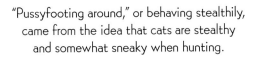

"Pussyfooting around," or behaving stealthily, came from the idea that cats are stealthy and somewhat sneaky when hunting.

Showing anger, or "getting one's back up" comes from the behavior of cats, who set their backs up when attacked by dogs or other animals.

The cat-o'-nine-tails was a whip made with nine tails with three or more knots per tail. This was used for various punishments,

both in political disputes and crimes. It left marks that looked like cat's claws.

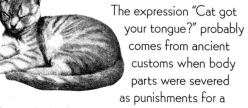

The expression "Cat got your tongue?" probably comes from ancient customs when body parts were severed as punishments for a specific misdeed. A liar's tongue was ripped out, rendering him unable to speak.

"Fat cat" is an idiom for a wealthy person.

The expression "There's more than one way to skin a cat" originated from preparing catfish for cooking. Catfish skin is tough and must be skinned using various methods.

Cat house is another name
for a house of ill-repute.

The gem Cat's Eye has a changeable
luster and the power to shine like
a cat's eye.

Pussy willow trees, also know at catkins, are
said to have gotten their names from a Polish legend
that says that a willow tree once saw
a mother cat crying over her kittens
which had been thrown into the water
to drown. The willow dragged its low
branches in the water so that the kittens
could be saved. Ever since then,
willows put out little "kittens"
of velvety fur each spring

Red Barber, radio broadcaster
for the Brooklyn Dodgers, made
popular the expression "sitting
in the catbird seat," which means
sitting in a position of advantage
or prominence.

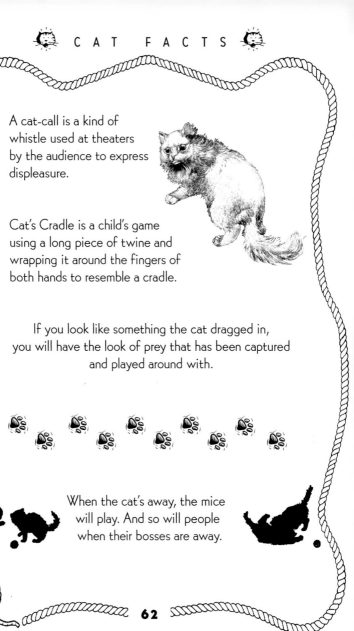

A cat-call is a kind of whistle used at theaters by the audience to express displeasure.

Cat's Cradle is a child's game using a long piece of twine and wrapping it around the fingers of both hands to resemble a cradle.

If you look like something the cat dragged in, you will have the look of prey that has been captured and played around with.

When the cat's away, the mice will play. And so will people when their bosses are away.

Grinning like a cheshire cat is an expression that comes from Lewis Carroll's famous Cheshire Cat in *Alice's Adventures in Wonderland*.

English proverb: All cats are gray in the dark.

Italian proverb: The cat loves fish, but hates wet feet.

Irish proverb: Beware of people who dislike cats.

Albanian proverb: A cat is a lion to a mouse.

German proverb: To live long, eat like a cat, drink like a dog.

Japanese proverb: The borrowed cat catches no mice.

Chinese proverb: A lame cat is better than a swift horse when rats infest the palace.

Arabic proverb: A cat that is always crying catches no mice.

A catnap, the slang expression for a short nap, developed from the cat's ability to sleep frequently and lightly for short periods of time.